Plastic Canvas

COASTERS AND LOLLIPOP COVERS

Stitch up these divine designs!

2

5

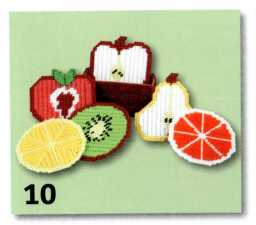
10

15

20

24

28

LEISURE ARTS, INC. • Maumelle, Arkansas

WATERMELON COASTERS

WHO DOESN'T LOVE a fresh slice of watermelon on a hot summer day? Serve up these cute coasters at your next picnic.

COASTER (STITCH 6)
29 × 30 threads

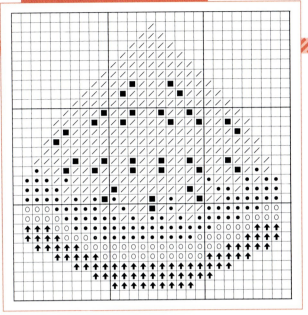

HOLDER UPPER SIDES (STITCH 2)
13 × 10 threads

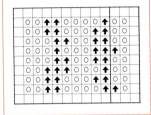

HOLDER LOWER SIDES (STITCH 2)
13 × 13 threads

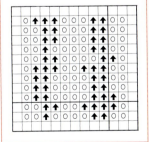

Note: Please read all instructions on page 32 before beginning.

COLOR KEY

- ■ Black
- ／ Dark Red
- ↑ Green
- ○ Lime Green
- ● Rose

Overcast the edges of the coasters using yarn that matches adjacent stitches.

Join the holder together and overcast the edges using Lime Green yarn.

3

HOLDER BOTTOM
17 × 13 threads

HOLDER FRONT AND BACK
(STITCH 2)
35 × 17 threads

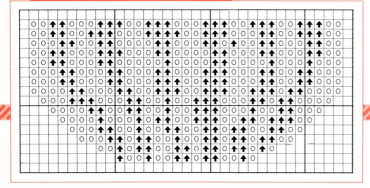

Note: Please read all instructions on page 32 before beginning.

COLOR KEY

- ■ Black
- ╱ Dark Red
- ↑ Green
- ○ Lime Green
- ● Rose

Overcast the edges of the coasters using yarn that matches adjacent stitches.

Join the holder together and overcast the edges using Lime Green yarn.

CUPCAKE COASTERS

THESE DELICIOUS DESIGNS make the perfect addition to your kitchen décor! The scrumptious coasters stitch up quickly and will add charm to your home.

5

COASTER 1
35 × 34 threads

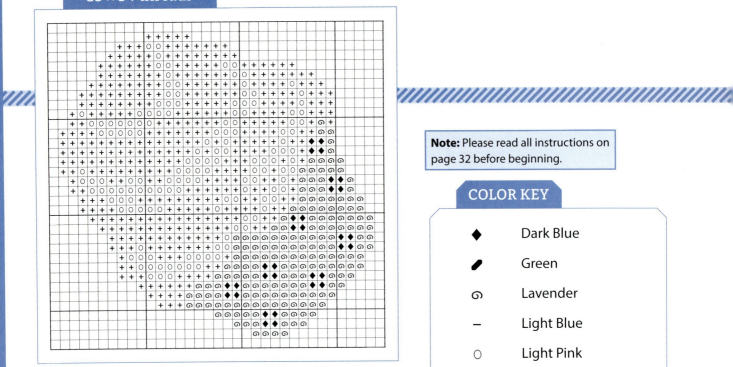

Note: Please read all instructions on page 32 before beginning.

COLOR KEY

◆	Dark Blue
✎	Green
૭	Lavender
—	Light Blue
○	Light Pink
△	Lime Green
·	Orange
+	Red
↑	Yellow

Overcast the edges of the coasters using yarn that matches adjacent stitches.

Join the holder together and overcast the edges using Light Blue yarn.

COASTER 2
35 × 34 threads

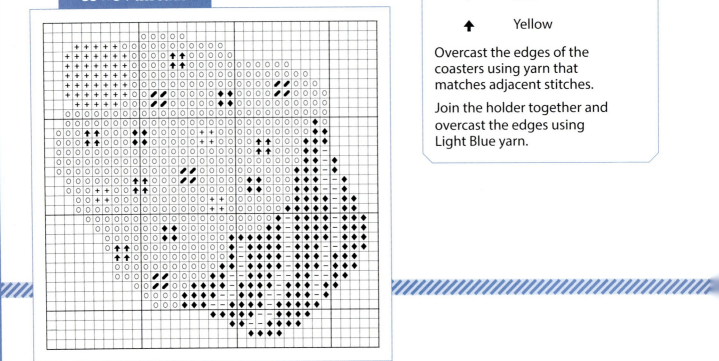

COASTER 4
35 × 34 threads

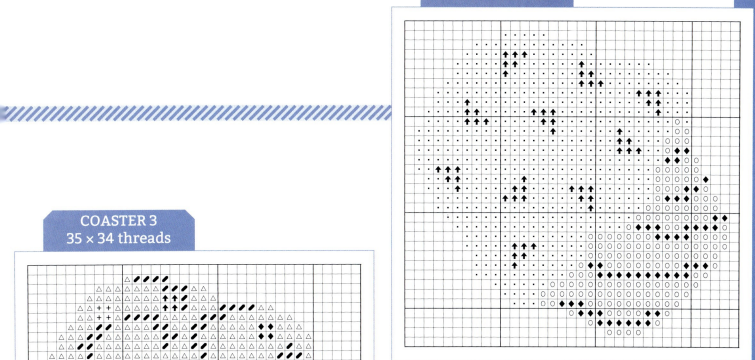

COASTER 3
35 × 34 threads

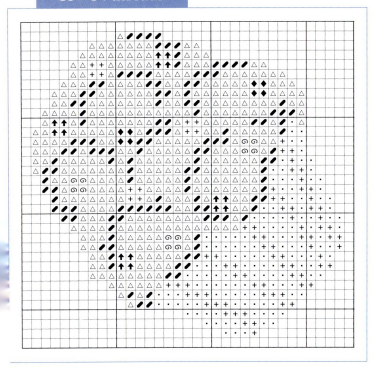

COASTER 5
35 × 34 threads

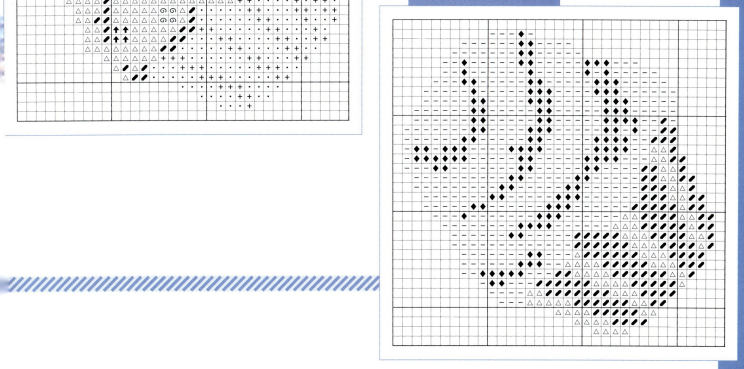

7

COASTER 6
35 × 34 threads

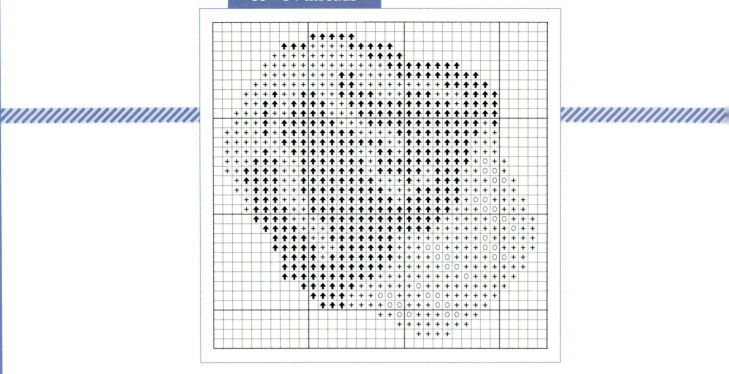

Note: Please read all instructions on page 32 before beginning.

COLOR KEY

- ♦ Dark Blue
- ◗ Green
- ၅ Lavender
- — Light Blue
- ○ Light Pink
- △ Lime Green
- · Orange
- + Red
- ↑ Yellow

Overcast the edges of coasters using yarn that matches adjacent stitches.

Join the holder together and overcast the edges using Light Blue yarn.

PROJECT TIP

It is best to work with at least one-yard cuts of yarn when stitching your plastic canvas item. You can use longer cuts for larger areas of the same color, as this will avoid too many stops and starts with the same color.

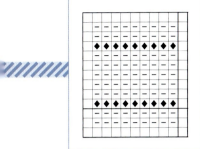

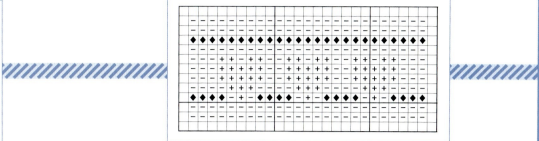

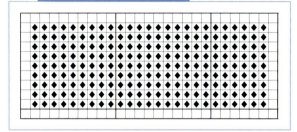

FRUIT SLICE COASTERS

BRIGHT, MOUTHWATERING DESIGNS are ideal for summer! These juicy coasters will keep your tables spot-free while adding a pop of color.

Note: Please read all instructions on page 32 before beginning.

COLOR KEY

■	Black
♦	Bright Yellow
♥	Dark Red
▲	Lime Green
★	Medium Brown
◖	Pale Yellow
၅	Rose
✳	White

Straight Stitch (Yarn)

～～～	Bright Yellow
⊥⊥⊥⊥⊥	Green
———	Lime Green
▬·▬·▬	Orange
▬·•·▬	Rose
———	White

A symbol charted at the intersection of two bars represents the center of your stitch. Bring the needle up through the hole to the bottom left of the symbol and slant up to the right, bringing the needle down through the hole to the top right of the symbol.

Make straight stitches in the color indicated, bringing the needle up through the hole at one end of the line and back down through the hole at the other end of the line, following the direction and length of the line as shown on the chart.

Overcast the coasters using yarn that matches adjacent stitches.

Join the holder together and overcast the edges using Medium Brown yarn.

STRAWBERRY
30 × 31 threads

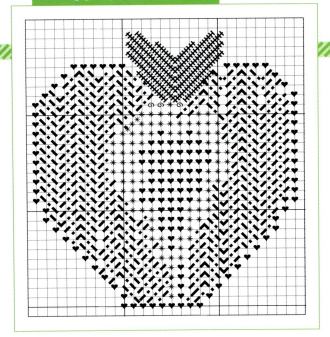

LEMON
29 × 29 threads

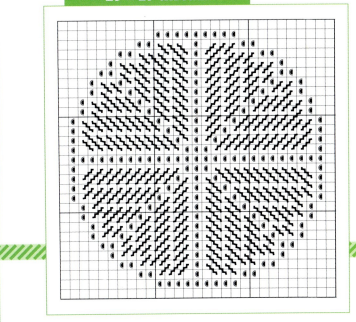

11

Note: Please read all instructions on page 32 before beginning.

KIWI
30 × 31 threads

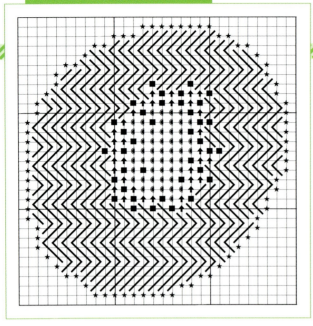

APPLE
29 × 32 threads

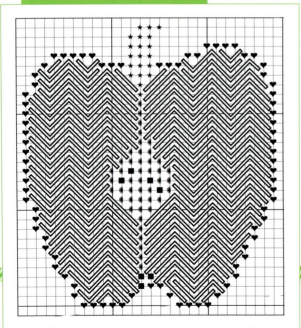

COLOR KEY

■	Black
♦	Bright Yellow
♥	Dark Red
↑	Lime Green
★	Medium Brown
◖	Pale Yellow
ତ	Rose
✳	White

Straight Stitch (Yarn)

ᴡᴡᴡᴡ	Bright Yellow
⊢⊢⊢⊢	Green
────	Lime Green
─▬─▬─	Orange
·─·─·─	Rose
═══	White

A symbol charted at the intersection of two bars represents the center of your stitch. Bring the needle up through the hole to the bottom left of the symbol and slant up to the right, bringing the needle down through the hole to the top right of the symbol.

Make straight stitches in the color indicated, bringing the needle up through the hole at one end of the line and back down through the hole at the other end of the line, following the direction and length of the line as shown on the chart.

Overcast the coasters using yarn that matches adjacent stitches.

Join the holder together and overcast the edges using Medium Brown yarn.

PEAR
30 × 33 threads

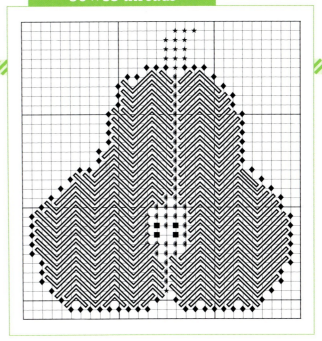

PROJECT TIP

If you accidentally cut through a canvas bar, you can put a small scrap piece of plastic canvas behind the mistake and stitch through both layers.

ORANGE
29 × 29 threads

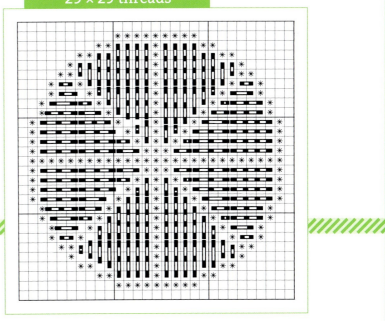

HOLDER FRONT AND BACK (STITCH 2)
33 × 18 threads

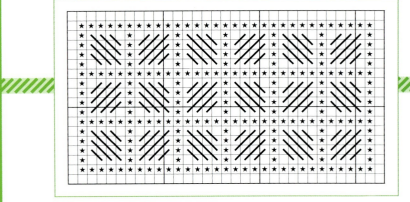

HOLDER BOTTOM
33 × 13 threads

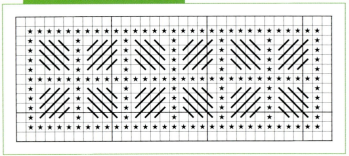

HOLDER SIDES (STITCH 2)
13 × 18 threads

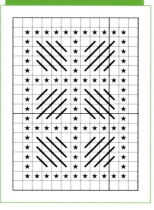

COLOR KEY

★   Medium Brown

Scotch Stitch—used on holder with Medium Brown yarn.

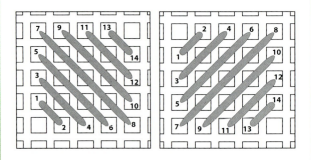

Join the holder together and overcast the edges using Medium Brown yarn.

Note: Please read all instructions on page 32 before beginning.

PEPPERMINT COASTERS

A FAVORITE CHRISTMAS CANDY looks super sweet as coasters! Bring out these vibrant designs at your next holiday gathering.

COASTER 1
31 × 31 threads

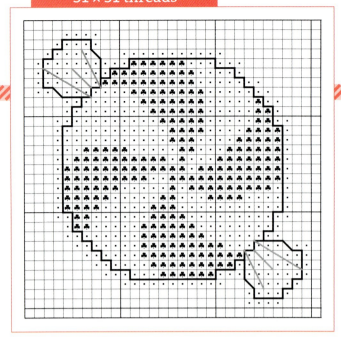

COASTER 2
31 × 31 threads

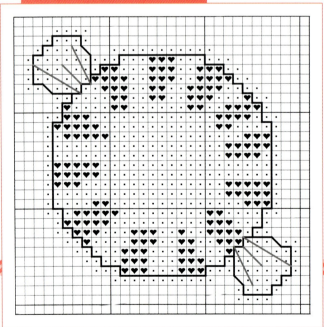

Note: Please read all instructions on page 32 before beginning.

COLOR KEY

↑	Green
ෆ	Light Pink
♣	Lime Green
♥	Red
·	White

Backstitch Floss (4 strands)

——— Black

Straight Stitch Floss (4 strands)

——— Black

Overcast the edges of the coasters using White yarn.

Join holder together and overcast the edges using Green yarn.

COASTER 3
31 × 31 threads

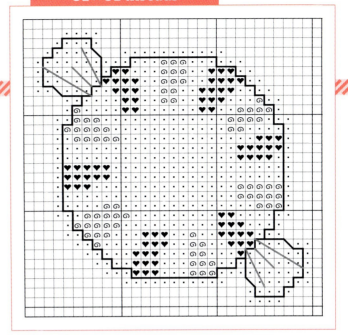

PROJECT TIP

Save your leftover scraps of plastic canvas in a small box. You never know when a future project will need small pieces of plastic canvas! Scraps are also great for practicing new stitches or experimenting with color combinations.

COASTER 4
31 × 31 threads

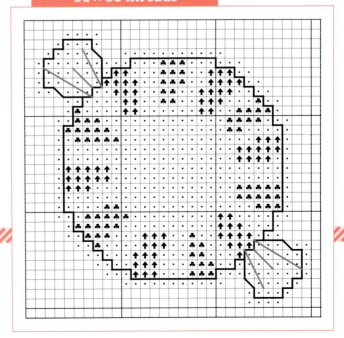

17

COASTER 5
31 × 31 threads

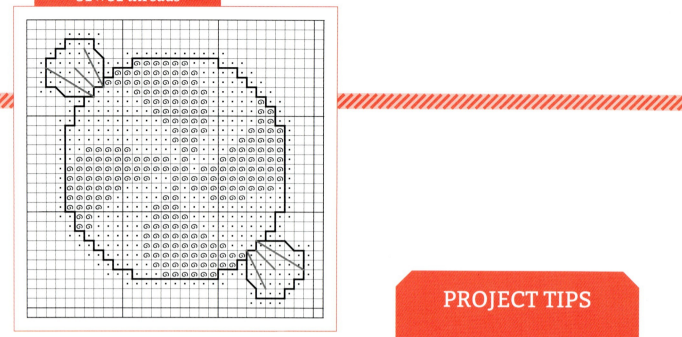

PROJECT TIPS

When you end a section of stitching or finish a thread, weave the yarn through the back side of your last few stitches, then trim it off.

Work embroidery stitches over needlepoint stitches after the canvas piece is filled in.

COASTER 6
31 × 31 threads

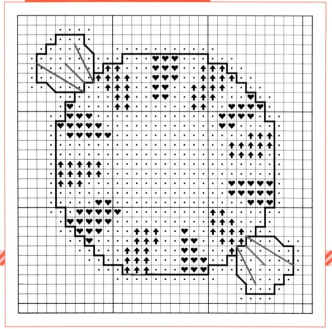

HOLDER BOTTOM
32 × 32 threads

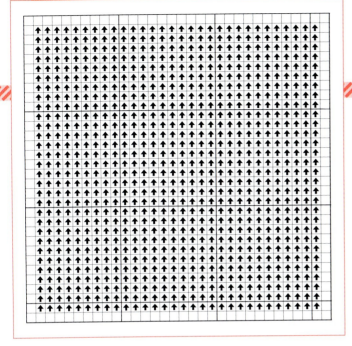

Note: Please read all instructions on page 32 before beginning.

COLOR KEY

↑	Green
๑	Light Pink
♣	Lime Green
♥	Red
·	White

Backstitch Floss (4 strands)

――― Black

Straight Stitch Floss (4 strands)

――― Black

Overcast the edges of the coasters using White yarn.

Join holder together and overcast the edges using Green yarn.

HOLDER FRONT, BACK, AND SIDES (STITCH 4)
32 × 13 threads

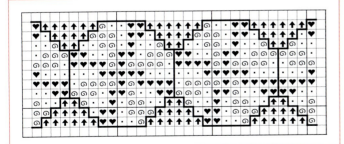

19

SPOOKY FRIENDS LOLLIPOP COVERS

NO TRICKS HERE—only treats! Whether decorating a table with these during a Halloween party or giving them as gifts to trick-or-treaters, these spook-tacular lollipop covers will be adored by ghouls and goblins of all ages!

PIRATE
38 × 38 threads

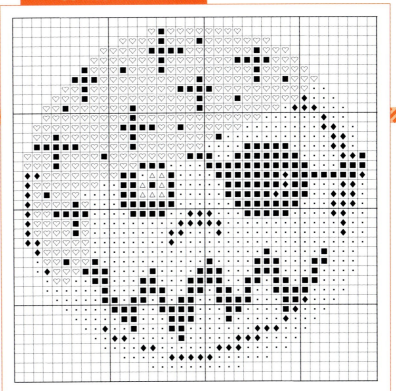

Note: Please read all instructions on page 32 before beginning.

COLOR KEY

■	Black
▬	Green
✳	Lavender
◆	Light Gray
△	Lime Green
╱	Orange
♡	Red
·	White
+	Yellow

Backstitch (Yarn)

——— Black

Overcast the edges using yarn that matches the adjacent stitches.

MUMMY
38 × 38 threads

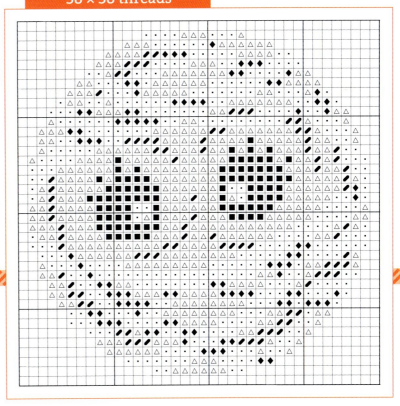

PUMPKIN
38 × 38 threads

Note: Please read all instructions on page 32 before beginning.

COLOR KEY

■	Black
◗	Green
✷	Lavender
◆	Light Gray
△	Lime Green
╱	Orange
♡	Red
·	White
+	Yellow

Backstitch (Yarn)

―― Black

Overcast the edges using yarn that matches the adjacent stitches.

SPIDERWEB
38 × 38 threads

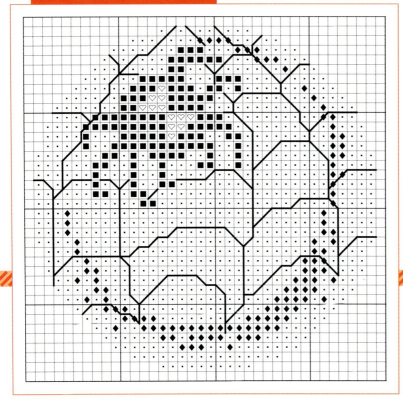

WITCH
40 × 39 threads

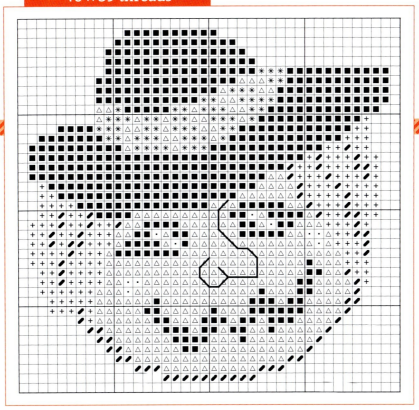

GHOST
38 × 38 threads

23

CHRISTMASTIME LOLLIPOP COVERS

TREAT YOUR LOVED ONES to these adorable lollipop covers! They'll love finding one in their stocking on Christmas morning.

POLAR BEAR
39 × 39 threads

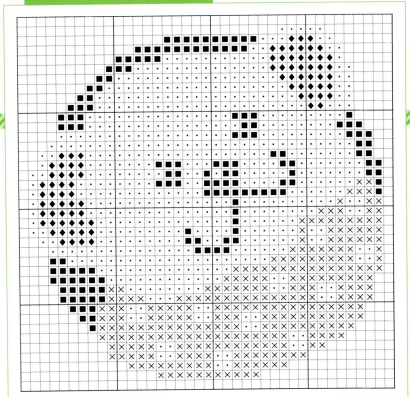

Note: Please read all instructions on page 32 before beginning.

COLOR KEY

■	Black
╱	Dark Blue
×	Green
◣	Light Gray
✱	Orange
▐	Red
◆	Rose
T	Sand
◇	Tan
·	White
●	Yellow

Backstitch (Yarn)

——— Black

Overcast the edges using yarn that matches the adjacent stitches.

SNOWMAN WITH STRIPED SCARF
41 × 40 threads

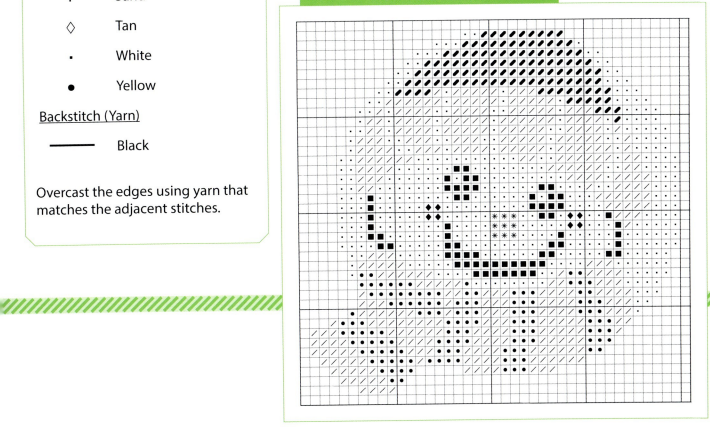

PENGUIN
39 × 38 threads

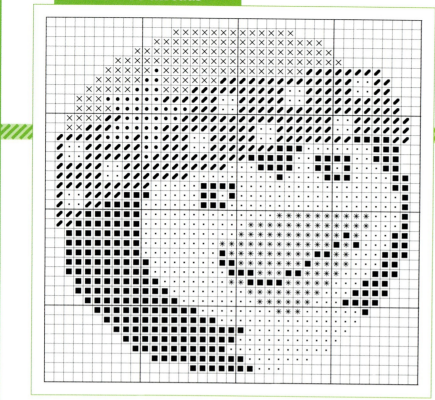

REINDEER
38 × 39 threads

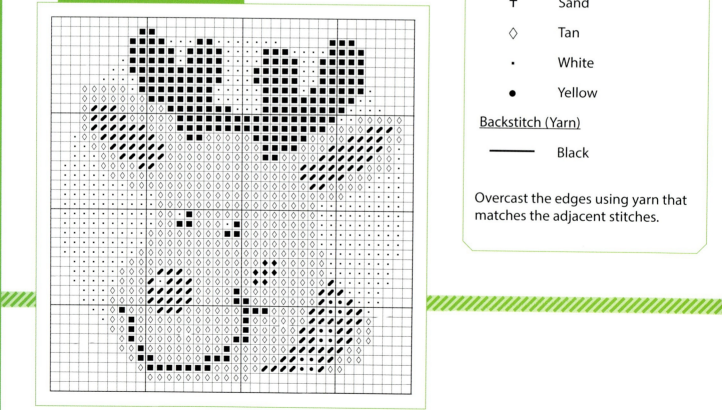

Note: Please read all instructions on page 32 before beginning.

COLOR KEY

■	Black
╱	Dark Blue
×	Green
◣	Light Gray
✻	Orange
⬤	Red
◆	Rose
⊤	Sand
◇	Tan
·	White
●	Yellow

<u>Backstitch (Yarn)</u>

——— Black

Overcast the edges using yarn that matches the adjacent stitches.

SNOWMAN WITH BLACK HAT
40 × 39 threads

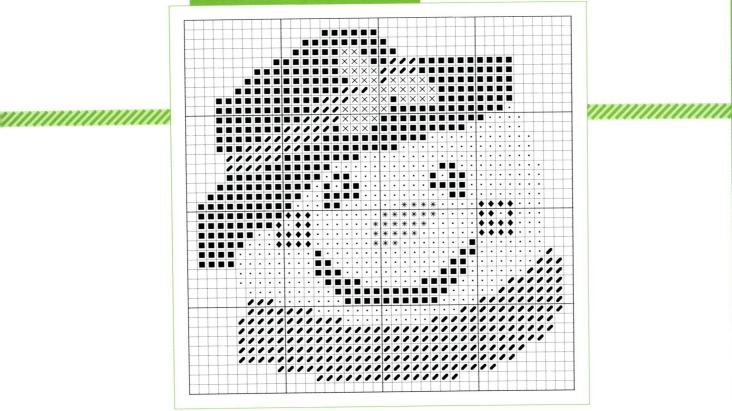

SANTA
38 × 38 threads

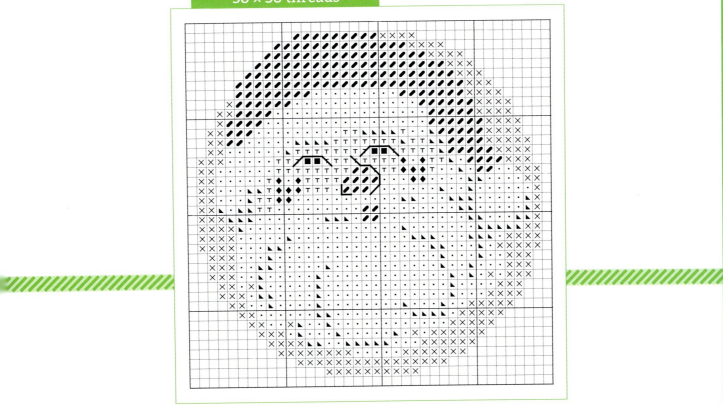

EASTER LOLLIPOP COVERS

EVERYONE WILL HAVE a "Hoppy Easter" with these fun lollipop covers! Whether adding them to an Easter basket or hiding them for little ones to find, everyone will adore these delightful designs.

Note: Please read all instructions on page 32 before beginning.

COLOR KEY

- ■ Black
- + Bright Yellow
- ○ Dark Blue
- — Dark Purple
- v Green
- ▶ Lavender
- ◆ Light Blue
- ✱ Light Brown
- ✿ Light Gray
- ★ Light Peach
- ● Light Pink
- ♣ Lime Green
- ✖ Orange
- ♡ Rose
- ♠ Rust
- ╱ Tan
- · White
- ↑ Yellow

<u>Backstitch Floss (4 strands)</u>

- ─── Black

Overcast the edges using yarn that matches the adjacent stitches.

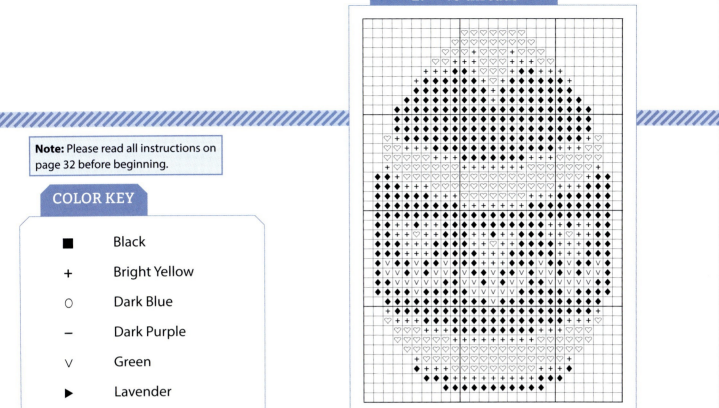

BLUE EGG
27 × 40 threads

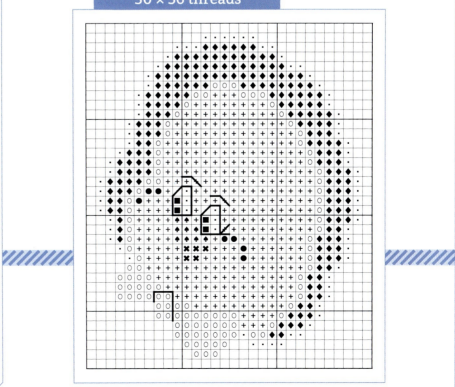

CHICK
30 × 36 threads

DUCK
31 × 33 threads

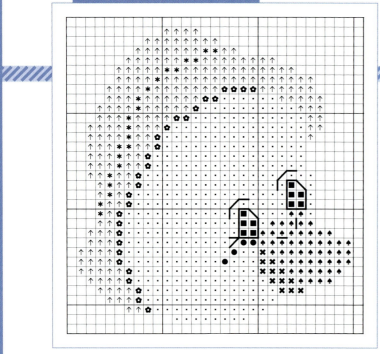

Note: Please read all instructions on page 32 before beginning.

COLOR KEY

■	Black
+	Bright Yellow
○	Dark Blue
—	Dark Purple
∨	Green
▶	Lavender
◆	Light Blue
✱	Light Brown
✿	Light Gray
★	Light Peach
●	Light Pink
♣	Lime Green
✖	Orange
♡	Rose
♠	Rust
╱	Tan
·	White
↑	Yellow

Backstitch Floss (4 strands)

—— Black

Overcast the edges using yarn that matches the adjacent stitches.

LAMB
31 × 34 threads

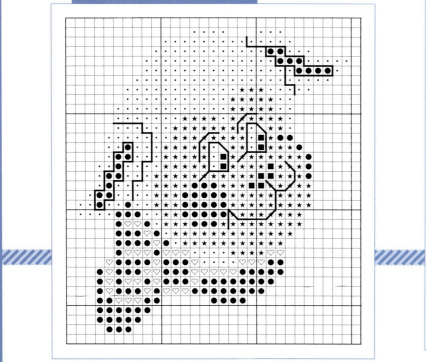

RABBIT
32 × 37 threads

PROJECT TIP

Nail clippers work great for cutting off the little nubs of plastic canvas left over when you cut out a pattern piece. These nubs can snag your yarn, so it's best to get the edge as smooth as possible.

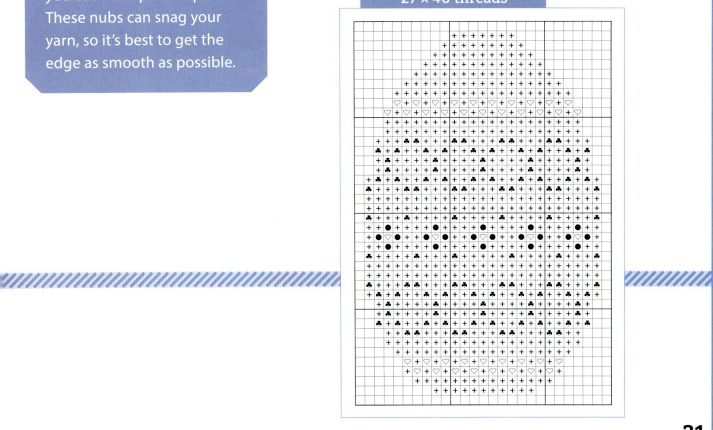

YELLOW EGG
27 × 40 threads

COASTERS AND LOLLIPOP COVERS

GENERAL INSTRUCTIONS

QUICK TIPS
1. Prior to beginning a project, look over the requirements and directions carefully.
2. Stitch the design on an uncut piece of plastic canvas to avoid snagging yarn or floss on ragged edges. If necessary, cover the edge with masking tape to avoid snags.
3. For a finished look, trim rough edges and cut off corners at an angle.
4. All pieces are stitched on 7-mesh plastic canvas using a size 16 tapestry needle and worsted weight yarn. Floss details use 4 strands of cotton embroidery floss.

STARTING TO STITCH
All stitches begin on the back of your work. With a threaded needle, come up from the back of your work, hold a 1" section of the yarn against the back of the canvas and stitch over the 1" section. This will eliminate the need for a knot on the end of your yarn and will keep the back side of your work clean and flat. To finish off a color, run the needle under 4 or 5 stitches on the back and clip off. The tension of the stitches will hold the yarn in place and knots will not be necessary.

DIRECTIONS
- Stitch the piece(s). Except where otherwise indicated, ½ cross stitch is used for all main areas.
- To work the charts, start with the top left stitch using the yarn color indicated on the chart and color key. Bring the needle up from the back of the work at the symbol indicated to create the first stitch (see diagram).
- Cut away surplus canvas. Cut outside and trim the rough edges next to unworked edges. Overcast all edges with matching adjacent color.

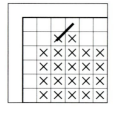

CUTTING YOUR CANVAS
Always cut your canvas between the bars, making sure to leave one plastic bar between the stitches and cutting line. By cutting between the bars, you will be assured an adequate amount of plastic for overcasting the edges when finishing (see diagram).

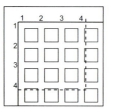

CLEANING
Hand-wash plastic canvas projects in warm water with a mild soap. Do not rub or scrub stitches, as this will cause the yarn to fuzz. Do not put your stitched piece in the dryer; allow to air dry.

LOLLIPOP COVER FINISHING
Glue felt to the back of the project, placing glue around the outer edges and leaving the bottom open to insert a lollipop. The width of the opening may vary due to the size of the lollipop.

STITCH GUIDE

½ Cross Stitch
Most commonly used, it is either stitched in rows or columns. This stitch slants up from left to right. Always bring the needle up on odd numbers and down on even numbers.

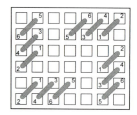

Overcast Stitch
This stitch is used for finishing your edges or joining two pieces of canvas. The stitch comes up in one hole, over the border bar and up the next hole, over the border bar and up the next hole.

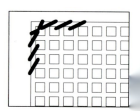

Backstitch
A backstitch is made in any direction with multiple continuous stitches crossing one bar at a time.

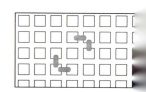

Straight Stitch
A straight stitch is formed by bringing the needle up at 1 and down at 2. The stitch can be of any length and worked in any direction.

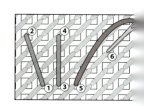

Produced by Herrschners, Inc., for distribution exclusively by Leisure Arts, Inc., 104 Champs Blvd., STE 100, Maumelle, AR 72113-6738, leisurearts.com.

Copyright © 2015 by Herrschners, Inc. All rights reserved. This publication is protected under federal copyright laws. Reproduction of this publication or any other Leisure Arts publication, including publications which are out of print, is prohibited unless specifically authorized. This includes, but is not limited to, any form of reproduction or distribution on or through the Internet, including posting, scanning, or e-mail transmission.

We have made every effort to ensure that these instructions are accurate and complete. We cannot, however, be responsible for human error, typographical mistakes, or variations in individual work.